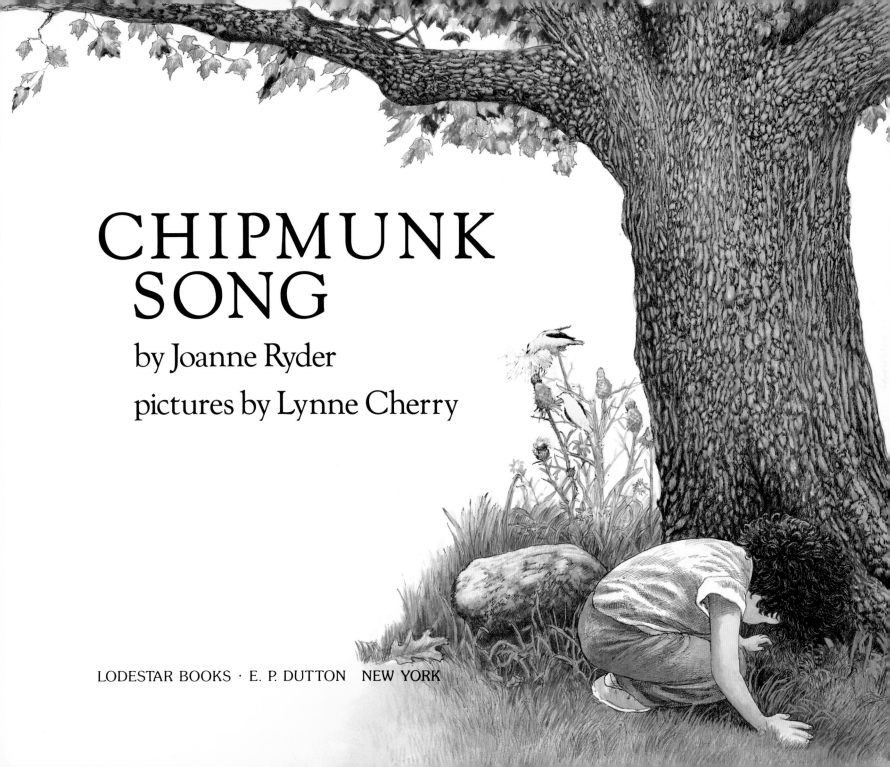

CHIPMUNK SONG

by Joanne Ryder

pictures by Lynne Cherry

LODESTAR BOOKS · E. P. DUTTON   NEW YORK

Acknowledgement is due to the scientific reports
of chipmunk behavior, especially Lawrence Wishner's
lively and thorough study, *Eastern Chipmunks: Secrets
of Their Solitary Lives,* Smithsonian Institution
Press (Washington, D.C., 1982).

Text copyright © 1987 by Joanne Ryder
Illustrations copyright © 1987 by Lynne Cherry

Library of Congress Cataloging-in-Publication Data
Ryder, Joanne.
    Chipmunk song.
    "Lodestar books."
    Summary: A lyrical description of a chipmunk as it
goes about its activities in late summer, prepares for
winter, and settles in till spring.
    1. Chipmunks—Juvenile literature.   [1. Chipmunks]
I. Cherry, Lynne, ill.   II. Title.
QL737.R68R9   1987   599.32'32   86-19786
ISBN 0-525-67191-9

Published in the United States by E. P. Dutton,
2 Park Avenue, New York, N.Y. 10016

Published simultaneously in Canada by
Fitzhenry & Whiteside Limited, Toronto

Editor: Virginia Buckley   Designer: Riki Levinson

Printed in Hong Kong by South China Printing Co.
First Edition   COBE   10 9 8 7 6 5 4 3 2 1

to Annette, my friend and cousin, with love

J. R.

to Dad, who taught me to love the critters,
and Mom, who encouraged me to draw them

L. C.

Under the trees
under the grass
deep in the ground
small ones live
in darkness.

Imagine
you are someone small
sleeping on a bed of leaves
in a cool, dark room
underground.
Wake up, small one.

You cannot see
the sun,
but you feel
the morning stir
inside you.

Running
through a tunnel
just your size,
you climb
up and up
toward a circle
of brightness
above you.

At the edge
of your dark world,
you wait and listen
to birds
calling softly
to each other,
telling you
they feel safe.

You stretch
your furry head
up and out
into brightness
all around you.
You look
this way
and
that way
for danger
leaping
or creeping
or flying
toward you.
But no one
is coming.

So you run—
dashing quickly
stopping here
    stopping there
looking for food
watching for danger.
You are fast—
leaping over a rock
scooting under a bush
where the last
bright berries hang.
You stretch up high
to eat the sweet berries,
grasping each one
in your furry paws.

At the old wall,
you leap up
from stone to stone to stone
and sit under the trees,
looking at your bright world.

chip chip chip chip chip
You sing a song.
Other small ones
hear it too
and begin to sing
chip chip chip chip
and you know
you are not alone.

Headfirst
you climb down
to the brown ground
where the sunlight
makes bright stripes
in the shade.

You are brown
like the dry leaves
like the brown earth
around you.
You are brown
and soft and furry.
Light and dark stripes
mark your furry face
your furry body
your long furry tail.

A black shadow
glides across the ground.
You lie still
like a brown statue
on the brown ground
till hawk
floats over the trees
without seeing you.

Then you run.
thump thump thump thump thump thump
Your heart beats as fast
as a tiny clock inside you.

You run to a place
where fat acorns have fallen.
You stuff an acorn
inside your furry cheek.
Then another
        and another
                and another!

Like fat pockets
your cheeks puff—
full of acorns.
You race home,
your long furry tail
trailing behind
till you disappear
into a small hole
in the grass.

When you come up,
your cheeks are empty.
You sit in the warm sun
and lick your paws
to wash your dirty face.
You lick clean
your long furry tail.

All day long
you run to the woods,
filling your cheeks
with acorns
to hide in your home
underground.

As the days grow cooler,
the birds fly away
to warmer places.
But you stay,
carrying food
from the bright world
to your dark home.

Each day
red leaves and
brown leaves and
yellow leaves
fall from the trees.
You carry some
to your nest,
biting them
into colorful pieces,
making a warmer bed
to sleep in.

But one cold day
you stay inside
your dark tunnel.
You fill your
bright doorway
with dirt.
Far above you,
weasel hunts
but finds
no hole
in the grass.

Under the bare trees
under the cold snow
deep in the ground
small ones sleep
in darkness.

thump
thump
thump

Like a tiny drum
beating
softly
slowly
your heart
ticks away
the winter days
the winter nights
while you sleep.

Now and then
you uncurl
and stretch
your furry legs.
You dig
through leaves
and find
good things
under your bed.
In the darkness,
you eat
fat acorns
you cannot see.

Then,
too sleepy
to eat anymore,
you curl
into a furry ball
and rest.
Tucked inside
the safe earth,
you wait
for the warm days
of spring
to call you
up and up
to the bright world
above.